C000099539

SWALEDALE

Keith Wood

First published in Great Britain in 2010

British Library Cataloguing-in-Publication Data
A CIP record for this title is available from the British Library

ISBN 978 1 906887 87 2

PiXZ Books
Halsgrove House, Ryelands Industrial Estate,
Bagley Road, Wellington, Somerset TA21 9PZ
Tel: 01823 653777
Fax: 01823 216796
email: sales@halsgrove.com

An imprint of Halstar Ltd, part of the Halsgrove group of companies
Information on all Halsgrove titles is available at: www.halsgrove.com

Printed and bound in China by Toppan Leefung Printing Ltd

Contents

How to use this book

Swaledale, the most northerly of the principal Yorkshire Dales, offers great walking opportunities for either the experienced walker or those seeking a gentle stroll along the valley floor. Rising high in the Pennines, the river flows east towards Richmond, before turning south around Catterick, its waters eventually joining those of the Ure and Ouse before flowing into the North Sea through the Humber Estuary. This collection of walks is concentrated along Upper Swaledale between Keld and Reeth. Although the main tourist spots of Muker and Reeth can be busy at peak times, quiet footpaths and bridleways are quickly reached and the tranquillity of the area can be truly appreciated.

The hills around Swaledale are scarred and pockmarked from mining activity. Production reached its peak in the mid nineteenth century when thousands of tons of ore were brought to the surface. However, decline was to quickly follow, as the costs of production spiralled due to having to mine deeper and production came to halt at the turn of the twentieth century. In the eighteenth and nineteenth centuries this must have been a frightful, noisy and dirty place with smoke and fumes belching from the smelt mills above the valleys. Now all is quiet and the most likely disturbance is a group of walkers with their boots pounding along the old mine and quarry tracks.

The majority of walks in this book are easy to moderate and offer pleasant walking in this beautiful and varied landscape. For the more adventurous Kisdon and Great Pinseat (walks 2 and 8) give a taste of the higher fell walking available.

Each route is graded from Easy to More Challenging with further details of distance, height ascended and the type of terrain covered, to help with decisions of which walk to choose. The information blocks have distances and height gained in both imperial and metric measures, whereas in the body of the text I have kept to the old imperial units which still feel more appropriate (and comfortable) when describing the walks. The majority of the walks have details of refreshments and facilities available – usually at the end, however for some this requires a minor detour or short car journey.

All ten walks are covered by the Ordnance Survey Explorer Map OL: 30Yorkshire Dales, Northern and Central areas, and Harvey's Dales North maps. The maps in this book are only an outline version of each walk and the detail provided by the OS maps puts each route in context.

Every year tens of thousands of visitors enjoy the dales with the vast majority coming to no harm. However there are many cases each year where walkers are injured, get lost or find themselves in some other kind of difficulty requiring the assistance of the Rescue Services. A few simple precautions should help avoid any problems:

- If you are unsure about your fitness start with the walks graded Easy and work your way up to More Challenging.
- Wear suitable footwear – properly fitted walking boots are recommended for all the walks.
- Take suitable clothing; the weather in the Yorkshire Dales can change very quickly, take a waterproof and extra warm layers to wear.
- Take plenty to eat and drink en route, dehydration and lack of nourishment can lead to fatigue and mistakes being made.
- An outline map illustrates each walk but it is recommended that a complete map is taken.
- Inform someone of your planned route and expected return time.
- Check the weather forecast in advance and only take to the more challenging routes on clear days.
- Walks 1,5,8 and 10 pass evidence of mining activity along the way including a number of open levels. Do not be tempted to enter any of these – walking is strictly a surface pursuit!
- And finally keep to the paths and watch where you are putting your feet – most accidents are caused by careless slips!

Useful websites:

Yorkshire Dales National Park
www.yorkshiredales.org.uk

Yorkshire Dales Society
www.yds.org.uk

Yorkshire Dales Millennium Trust
www.ydmt.org

Out of Oblivion Yorkshire Dales Heritage and Archaeology
www.outofoblivion.org.uk

Yorkshire Dales Tourism
www.yorkshiredalesand harrogate.com

Traveldales – Public Transport Information
www.traveldales.org.uk

Keith Wood Photography
www.keithwoodphotography.co.uk

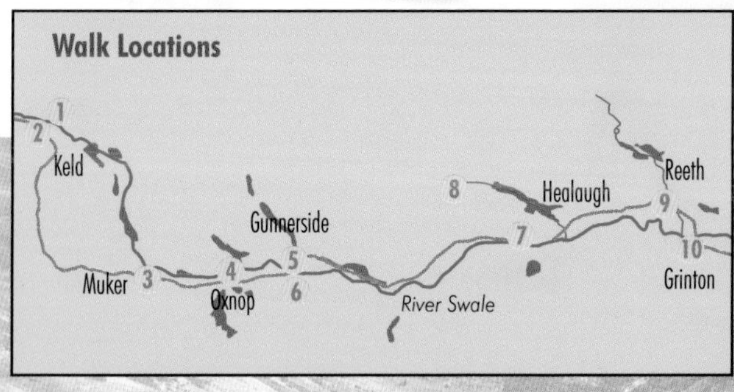

Key to Symbols Used

Level of difficulty:

Easy ♥
Fair ♥♥
More challenging ♥♥♥

Map symbols:

 Park & start
Tarred Road
Footpath
River
+ Church
Pub

1 Swinner Gill from Keld

A roller-coaster of a walk above the Swale to visit the remains of Swinner Gill Mines

Level: ♥ ♥
Length Miles and km: 3 ¾ m (6km)
Ascent feet and m: 950 feet (290m)
Terrain: Gentle ascents and descents on clear paths throughout
Park and Start: Park Lodge Farm Car Park in Keld GR892 012
Info: Toilets and refreshments available at the start

Keld is the nearest substantive habitation to the source of the Swale, although to use the word substantive may itself be misleading. Little more than a hamlet by today's standards, the majority of the public buildings date from the nineteenth century with the building of the United Reform Church, Chapel School and Village Institute. This development came a century after Keld's lead mining heyday when the nearby Beldi Hill and Swinner Gill lead mines were at their peak. This short walk from Keld passes by the remains of Beldi Hill Mines and the derelict Crackpot Hall on the way to visiting the more substantial remains of the Swinner Gill Lead Mines.

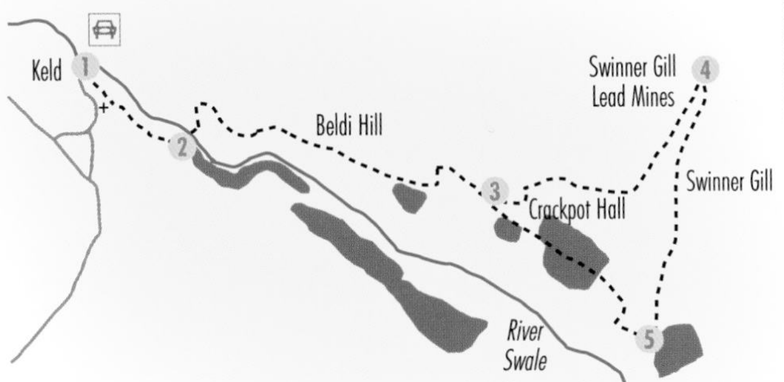

1 Leave the car park and walk back through the hamlet. Follow the "Public Footpath to Muker" sign straight on through the village onto an unsurfaced track heading along the valley. The hill to the front right is Kisdon. With the Swale tumbling along down in the gorge to the left the track narrows and the path on the opposite bank heading up to Crackpot Hall can be seen.

2 Where the path forks take the left hand path sign-posted "Pennine Way and Public Bridleway" which heads down to the valley bottom passing banks of wild garlic in the spring. Cross the wooden footbridge over the Swale and continue up the path on the opposite bank as it swings up the

East Gill Force, Keld

valley to the right with East Gill Force just on the right. Join the Public Bridleway and cross over the beck to start heading along Swaledale. The stony path rises up the hillside with the Swale in the valley bottom below on the right.

The bridleway levels giving a great view of Kisdon across the valley. The path follows a U shape around a well preserved stone barn and the remains of Beldi Hill Lead Mines can be seen up the valley on the left.

River Swale below Keld

3 At the remains of an old tractor the path forks; continue along the main lower path for a further 50 yards where the path forks again and this time take the upper left hand fork which continues to gently rise up the hillside. The ruins of Crackpot Hall are soon reached where the path rises to pass through the remains of lead mining activity and then swings to the right continuing to rise to another stone building. Pass the stone building and the path continues to rise. The path levels off as it swings around to the left to enter Swinner Gill. Go through a gate where the view now opens up along the steeply-sided Swinner Gill and the remains of Swinner Gill Lead Mines can be seen at the head of the valley. Continue along the narrowing

Crackpot Hall

high level path into the confines of Swinner Gill.

4 Approaching the head of the gill as the path swings around to head up to the remains of the mine workings a path signed "FP to Muker" doubles back heading down to the valley bottom on the same side of the gill. But first take the detour to inspect the abandoned mine workings. Head back to take the narrow path signed "FP Muker" heading back down the gill with the stream down below in the ravine to the left. Walking back along Swinner Gill the views open out along Swaledale. The path drops steeply down to the valley bottom and crosses Swinner Gill over a set of stepping stones before rising back up the opposite bank. A series of waterfalls are to be seen below on the right. Cross over a stile and continue on the narrow path as it proceeds along the valley heading towards the Swale. Approaching the end of the valley the path descends to meet the main bridleway between Muker and Keld.

5 Drop down to join the main bridleway; turn right and now follow this clear route following the Swale all the way back to Keld. The bridleway crosses back over Swinner

Swinner Gill Mines

Bridleway below Beldi Hill Mines

Gill either over the stepping stones or when in spate using the footbridge. Pass the lower mine workings before rising again up the hillside towards Keld. The bridleway passes by coppiced woodland as you rise studded with primroses and bluebells in the springtime. As height is gained and the view opens out Keld can be seen in the distance. The path levels off as the outward route is joined at the old tractor, and all that is now required is to retrace the steps of the outward journey back to the start.

The location of Crackpot Hall gives magnificent views along Swaledale. Surveys of the site have shown that its use has changed over the centuries and may have been a hunting lodge, a farm with cow sheds at each end, and possibly mine offices at the industrial height of the dale.

The fingerpost at the head of Swinner Gill

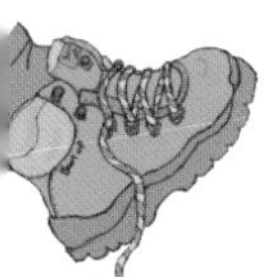

2 Kisdon and the Swale

A circuit of Kisdon and a visit to Kisdon Force

This second walk from the hamlet of Keld around Kisdon Hill gives the opportunity to gain an understanding of the geography of the upper dale with commanding views of the surrounding area. Kisdon is an isolated area of high ground with no ridges connecting to the adjacent fells. Wild flowers, including bluebells, abound on the eastern flanks of the hill in the spring. The River Swale makes its way around the eastern side of the hill, through a narrow ravine at the northern end before crashing over Kisdon Force. Approaching the village of Muker at the southern end of Kisdon, the Swale slows and the valley widens with green meadows on both banks.

Level:

Length Miles and km: 5 ¾ miles (9km)
Ascent feet and m: 1600 feet (480m)
Terrain: A long pull up Kisdon, followed by a riverside stroll
Park and Start: Park Lodge Farm Car Park in Keld GR892 012
Info: Toilets and refreshments available at the start

Wild garlic in the woods above the Swale

1 Start from the Park Lodge Farm Car Park at the bottom of Keld. Leave the car park and heading between the houses go back up to the main road. Pass the Keld United Reform Church and the former village hall where the road forks at the Public Conveniences take the left hand fork up to the main road. Upon meeting the main road along the valley at the War Memorial turn left with the green sides of Kisdon in sight on the left.

2 Walk down the beside the road to reach a walled farm track heading down to the left just in front of a field barn with a fingerpost "Bridleway Only to Muker 2 miles". Walk down the unsurfaced lane, cross over the strangely named Skeb Skeugh stream at the bottom. Pass through a gate and the track now starts to rise up the flanks of Kisdon. As height is gained pass through a gate onto the moor with great views now opening out across the dale to a patchwork of farms and field barns. The path continues to rise and passes through a second gate just beneath a lonely farmhouse. As a track turns off to the left to the farm the route continues straight on heading to a six bar gate on a green path. The green path continues to gently rise around the upper slopes of Kisdon. The natural quarry and cliffs of Swallow Hole are passed where the path

Slopes of Kisdon

straightens through a gate; follow the fingerpost sign to Muker. The route follows the remains of walled lane across the top of the hill. Leaving the walled lane behind the path heads over the top of Kisdon on open moorland. Passing through another gate the highest point of the route is reached at 1600 feet (485m) where to the left there are fine view into the depths of Swinner Gill.

3 The path now starts to descend down the slopes away from a wall towards Muker. As height is lost the view opens out along the length of Swaledale with Muker below and the patchwork of fields and barns. The path enters a walled lane. At a junction of paths at a pair of barns take the left fork to continue heading down the fellside and enter another walled lane still signed to Muker. The lane now joins an unsurfaced farm track which continues down the hillside towards Muker. Follow the lane as it zig zags down the hillside.

4 Approaching the valley bottom at a tight turn in the road to the right with a wall in front take the narrow lane to the left through a gate heading back up the

Angram from Kisdon

Walled lane across the top of Kisdon

Meadows beside the Swale

dale. This narrow lane follows the line of the Swale heading upstream with the flagged path through the pastures down below on the right. This is a charming narrow path through light woodland surrounded by an abundance of wild flowers including banks of bluebells and wild garlic under the trees in the spring. The path leaves the woodland and drops down to meet the main path heading up the valley towards Keld. Keep to the main path through the fields along the valley bottom with the cleft of Swinner Gill in the centre ground. In the spring banks of bluebells adorn the slopes of Kisdon. Approaching Swinner Gill the path through the meadows continues in a straight line cutting the corner off a bend in the river. The ruins of Crackpot Hall can be seen on the hillside ahead on the opposite bank of the Swale. Having passed some abandoned farms in the valley bottom the path starts to gently climb uphill away from the Swale and passes a pair of abandoned cottages. At a third ruined cottage a sign points to Keld and the path continues to gently rise above the Swale as the valley narrows heading to Kisdon Force. The path enters woodland as the valley sides grow steeper with banks of wild garlic, bluebells and primroses. As the path reaches a green platform at a junction of paths follow the directions along the Pennine Way to Keld. The path now starts to descend through the woods.

5 Just under a cliff a sign points "FP Kisdon Upper Force" along a narrow path to the right. It's definitely worth taking the detour to visit Kisdon Force; take the path down through the trees with the sound of the water getting louder. Take care on this narrow and occasionally slippery path as it descends to the valley bottom. Having visited the falls retrace your steps back up to the junction with the main path. From here it's a straightforward matter of walking along the clear path, following the route of the Pennine Way, above the Swale all the way back to Keld.

The route along the side of Kisdon follows a path known as 'The Corpse Way'. For centuries, corpses were carried in wicker coffins down Swaledale for burial in the consecrated ground at the church in Grinton. The journey took two days and was hazardous in winter and during floods.

Lead mines across the Swale from the slopes of Kisdon

Kisdon Force

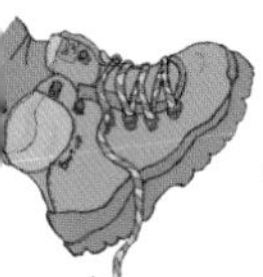

3 Muker to Ivelet Bridge

A gentle valley stroll, returning at a high level with outstanding views

Level:
Length Miles and km: 5½ miles (8.8km)
Ascent feet and m: 800 feet (240m)
Terrain: Easy walking with short uphill section through Ivelet
Park and Start: Car park by the bridge in Muker GR910 978
Info: Toilets, Farmers Arms pub, Teashop and Village Store in Muker

This delightful walk follows the northern bank of the Swale from the popular village of Muker down to Ivelet Bridge, the most impressive crossing of the Upper Swale before returning back up the dale on a higher level single track road. Muker has been an important settlement for centuries , its relative prosperity being built on agriculture, lead mining and knitting. Hand knitting was a commercial industry in the village in the mid nineteenth century and the village is still known for its knitwear available from Swaledale Woollens in the village.

The walk passes through the internationally important flower-rich Muker Hay Meadows on a stone flagged path to avoid damaging this sensitive environment.

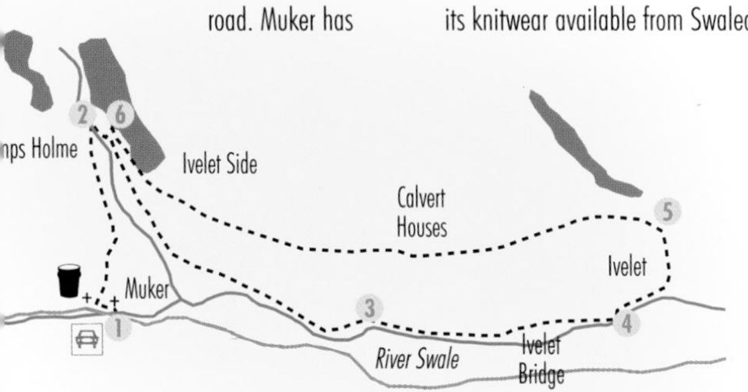

1 Park in the Richmondshire District Car Park at the east end of the village by the bridge over the Swale. Leave the car park and cross over the bridge into the village. Turn right and head up the lane in front of the Literary Institute through the back of the village. Pass the church, the Public Hall and Swale Farm and then follow the sign to "Gunnerside and Keld Meadowland Single file". Leave the buildings through a gate onto an unsurfaced lane into the open meadows. Follow the ancient paved path through the meadows; the ruins of Crackpot Hall can be seen on the hillside in the distance. Keep to the paved path passing a barn and through gated wall stiles across six or seven fields. The footbridge over the river comes into view on the right.

Barns in Muker Meadows

2 Passing through a final stile gate arrive at the riverside path; turn right signed "FP Gunnerside" to walk to the bridge. Cross the Swale over the narrow Ramps Holme wooden footbridge and at the far side immediately turn right following the footpath sign to Gunnerside on a muddy path following the course of the Swale. Just before a field barn the path forks; take the lower right path through a gate stile into the meadows to pass infront of Ramps Holme Farm. Look across the river for a view of Muker on the opposite bank. The route passes

through a series of haymeadows enclosed by the traditional drystone walls with a variety of stiles. Aim for the stile gate at the opposite side of each haymeadow and walk in single file through these important pastures. Pass a ford across the Swale and continue walking along the banks of the Swale as in meanders down the dale following the clear path along the riverbank.

The path enters some deciduous woodland at a bend in the river. Walk through the trees and leave the woodland through a gate back onto the path along the riverbank through the green pastures. Just past another field barn the path veers away from the river towards yet another gate stile where the path continues through the last pasture heading towards Ivelet Bridge.

River Swale above Muker

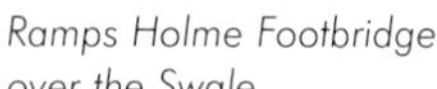

Ramps Holme Footbridge over the Swale

4 The path emerges onto the road at the impressive Ivelet Bridge. Follow the road straight on keeping to the left bank of the river. Follow the road as it starts to rise and swings away from the river towards the village of Ivelet. Keep straight on through Ivelet gaining height up the hillside. Cross over a cattle grid and keep heading up to pass the impressive Gunnerside Lodge. Keep to the road as it swings around the back of the lodge continuing to gain height.

Fields above the Swale

5 The road eventually levels off as it passes Ivelet Heads Cottage. Simply head back up the valley on the high level surfaced lane which gives outstanding views across the dale to Oxnop Gill. As the road forks above Calvert Houses continue on the upper lane. The road passes beneath the limestone of Kisdon Scar. As Muker comes back into sight the road starts to descend with Kisdon to the front right. The lane loses height heading towards the valley floor as the road swings around Ivelet Side and then loses its surface above Ramps Holme Farm.

Ivelet Bridge

6 Continue on the lane passing above Ramps Holme Footbridge and then look out for a path which doubles back to take you to the bridge to re-cross the Swale. All that remains is retrace the outbound route through the meadows back to the start at Muker.

Lead mining brought prosperity to Muker. The elaborate Literary Institute was built from public subscription in 1867 and originally contained a large library, a reading room with newspapers and a meeting room. The upper room is still in use as a practice room for Muker Silver Band.

The view up Swaledale from the high level road

4 Oxnop Gill

An exploration up one of the Swale's subsidiary valleys

Oxnop Beck is one of the main tributaries which flows into the Swale. Rising on the ridge which separates Swaledale from Wensleydale, the beck gathers pace down an occasionally steep sided ravine to join the Swale at the impressive Ivelet Bridge. This walk explores the lower reaches of the stream passing two attractive sets of waterfalls, before emerging on the open moorland at a higher level. After crossing the beck the route returns down the eastern side of the valley around the top of the now permanently dry (or blind) Spout Gill. As the route descends back down to Swaledale along Satron Side extensive views open up to the east and west along Swaledale.

Level: ♥♥

Length Miles and km: 3 miles (4.8km)

Ascent feet and m: 600 feet (180m)

Terrain: Steady rise up the gill.

Park and Start: Off road parking beside Ivelet Bridge GR 933 978

Info: No facilities on route

Ivelet across the valley

1 There are various parking spaces on the narrow road either side of Ivelet Bridge. Start by walking back up the narrow lane towards the main B6270 valley road with Oxnop Beck on the right hand side just before it joins the Swale.

2 Turn right and walk over Mill Bridge over Oxnop Beck. Immediately on the other side of the bridge go through the gap in the wall on the left, follow the "Footpath" fingerpost into the meadows to begin the journey beside Oxnop Beck up the valley. The faint green path heads up the bank through the first field and then enters the trees which border both sides of the beck. An impressive waterfall is shortly reached. The path continues to rise following the line of the beck and then rises more steeply

Falls along Oxnop Gill

Oxnop Hall

to pass by a large modern barn. Go through a pair of gates and continue to rise up the valley. The path passes the buildings of Low Oxnop Farm. The path goes through the fields skirting around the edge of the wood that line the beck to go through a wall stile into one last field before meeting the cross dale road. Cross the boggy pasture which is the source of a spring aiming for a farm gate through the wall to emerge onto the road.

3 Turn left and walk along the quiet narrow road with the views opening out up the valley to Oxnop Scar on the horizon. The road gently rises and at the first fingerpost "Footpath" on the left go over a stile to leave the road and re-enter the pastures to continue heading up the

Re-entering the fields from the road

valley. Steer diagonally towards the trees to cross the stream though the first field, follow the stream down for 20 yards where a gate through the wall leads onto a green track through the next field. Cross another stream heading down from High Oxnop Farm and through the next pasture to cross a fence at the apex of a finger of evergreen trees and continue to walk gently uphill with a drystone wall now on the right to the top of this next field. Go through a gate to arrive at the wooden footbridge across the top of Oxnop Beck.

4 Cross over the footbridge and continue on the path which rises up the beckside on the opposite bank. Climbing up above the beck the views up Swaledale open out. As the track rounds a bend a green path veers off to the left following the edge of the trees above the gill over a wooden stile over a fence. A narrow green path heads along the top of the deep ravine with the beck below. Keep a tight hold of children and dogs along this steep edge.

5 The path drops down to cross the blind (dry) Spout Gill and continues heading on to Gill Head Farm. The top of end of Spout Gill is a huge rabbit warren. The path becomes faint in places but keep straight along the valley through pastures aiming for the stiles at the end of each enclosure.

Upper Oxnop Gill

Footbridge across Oxnop Beck

6 The path reaches Gill Head Farm where an unsurfaced lane takes you onto the narrow single track lane where it's downhill all the way, simply following the narrow road all the way down to Satron. There are fine views up and down Swaledale with Ivelet and Gunnerside Lodge prominent on the opposite side of the valley.

Barn above Oxnop Beck

7 Upon reaching the main road at Satron, go straight across the road and take the green lane down the right of Satron Cottage. At the bottom follow the "FP" sign to Ivelet Bridge, through a gate and take the partially flagged path across the meadows heading back to the start. The path goes diagonally to the right through a second field heading

towards a farm and then down the back of the farm through another stile where the path drops down the bank to walk beside the riverside through the last field to Ivelet Bridge.

"What are you looking at?"

The single span high-arched bridge at Ivelet is thought by many to be the finest bridge over the Swale. Close by, a large flat stone is said to be where pall bearers placed the wicker coffins whilst taking a rest on their journey along the 'Corpse Way' to Grinton.

Wild Orchid in Oxnop Gill

5 Gunnerside Gill

An exploration of lead mining heritage deep into Gunnerside Gill

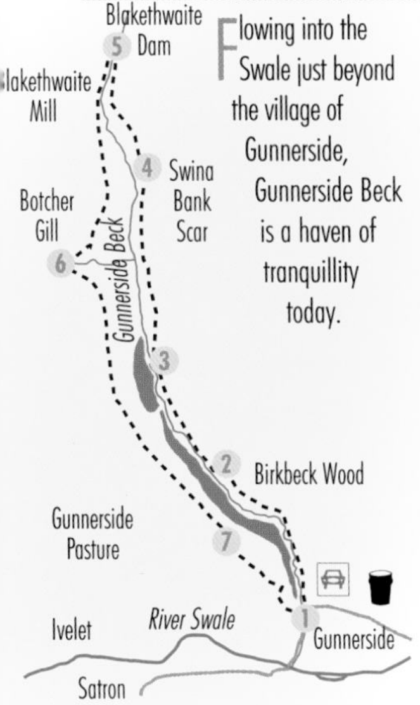

Flowing into the Swale just beyond the village of Gunnerside, Gunnerside Beck is a haven of tranquillity today.

Around 150 years ago the scene would have been very different with Gunnerside Gill being one of the centres of the lead mining industry in Swaledale. Smoke would be coming from the chimneys of the smelt mill up the valley. This walk follows in the footsteps of the miners, agents, surveyors and women and children who would have made the journey up from the village to the mines every day to work in the harshest of conditions. The route passes the remains of the Sir Frances Dressing Floor where lead ore was crushed and sorted prior to smelting and the Bunting Level which was the main access to the workings on the east side of Gunnerside Gill before reaching Blakethwaite Smelt Mill at the top of the walk. The route is a walk of two halves with a delightful tree-lined stroll along the lower reaches of the gill before gaining height to head up to the lead mining ruins.

Level: 🥾🥾
Length Miles and km: 6 miles (9.5km)
Ascent feet and m: 1300 feet (400m)
Terrain: Good paths throughout
Park and Start: Limited parking adjacent to Gunnerside Literary Institute GR950 982
Info: Refreshments from The Kings Head pub and Ghyll Tea Room in Gunnerside

(1) Park beside the beck outside Gunnerside's Literary Institute dating from 1877. Cross the bridge to the eastern bank of the beck and immediately follow the unsurfaced lane next to the beck signed "Footpath to Gunnerside Gill". It's an easy start to the walk walking beside the gill up to the private Gunnarsgill Hall. Just before the hall turn to the right up some steps to keep on the Public Footpath around the back of the hall and then proceed on a green path heading up the valley with the beck down on the left. Its a tranquil scene on the early stages of the walk keeping to path beside the tree lined beck. The "Gunnerside Gill Woodland Path" sign helpfully points the way through the trees where the path starts to rise up the steep sided valley above the water. It's a delightful path along the margins of Birkbeck Wood with a profusion of red-berried rowan or mountain ash in the late summer amongst the birch and hazel trees.

(2) Coming to the end of the wood the path dives down the gillside. Cross a planked bridge to arrive at the beckside path and the first sign of industrial activity as the

Gunnerside Beck

view up the valley opens out. Pop through the gate through the wall on the right and continue heading up the valley with the drystone wall now on the left. The preserved remains of lead mining activity at Sir Francis Dressing Floor is passed. The whole area surrounding this once industrialised zone is a giant rabbit warren. Continue up stream on the right bank of the beck with the next remains in sight.

Pop through the gate and continue heading up the valley

The Public Footpath goes over a stile and rises above the beck beside a wall. Passing a ruined building on the opposite bank the path now starts to gently rise up the valley side as the path continues up the gill.

3 For those in need of a shortcut ford the beck and continue back on the opposite bank – otherwise continue to walk up the valley. The path levels off and continues just above a wall. The ravine of Botcher Gill Nook is passed on the opposite bank. The heather on the higher levels becomes apparent. The path passes beneath Swinner Bank Scar with the Dolly Lead Level on the opposite bank.

Botcher Gill

Approaching a collection of preserved buildings high above the beck the view of the upper reaches of Gunnerside Gill opens out with its steep sides.

4 The path continues to rise past Bunton Mine to a four directional fingerpost. The route lies ahead to Blakethwaite Dam. Just beyond the sign the path forks; take the upper fork which continues at a high level above the beck. Approaching the head of the valley the green path now starts to gradually descend. Blakethwaite Mill is seen in the valley bottom and this will be visited shortly, but for the moment continue on the right bank.

The remains of Blakethwaite Dam with its waterfalls are

Gunnerside Gill

Looking down onto Blakethwaite Mill

soon reached which marks the furthest point of the journey up Gunnerside Gill. It's a little adventure to ford the gill over stepping stones to pick up the track on the opposite bank which takes you back to Blakethwaite Mill. And so begins the return trip on the western bank all the back to Gunnerside. Cross Blind Mill Beck at Blakethwaite Mill and take the clear track up the right hand bank of Gunnerside Gill rising up the hillside. The track rises above Lownathwaite Mines and passes through the North Hush and continues at a high level above the valley heading back down to Swaledale.

6 This fast high level path swings around the top of Botcher Gill. At the top of Botcher Gill the walkers' path joins a wide

unsurfaced track which continues heading along the valley. The view opens out to Swaledale. The track starts to gently lose height as it nears the end of the valley.

7 As the track swings around to the right a pile of stones marks the point to leave the track for a faint green path through the tussocky grass which makes a beeline for the village of Gunnerside. The path makes its way across some wet ground losing height all the time dropping down to the village. The path meets with a wire fence just above the village and simply follow it down into Gunnerside itself. Go through a gate to arrive back at the road just up from the start.

As production increased in Gunnerside, a new smelt mill was built at Blakethwaite. The two ore-hearths were fuelled by peat cut and dried on the high moorland and then stacked in an open-sided store by the mill. The peat store has been part of a stabilisation project in recent years.

The falls at the top of the walk

Blakethwaite Mill

6 Swale below Gunnerside

A gentle stroll along the banks of the Swale downstream from Gunnerside

This is the first of a pair of gentle riverside strolls alongside opposite banks of the Swale. Starting from the village of Gunnerside which dates from the late eighth century as a Norse settlement. The route makes use of two of the road bridges over the river. Initially crossing the steeply sloping Gunnerside New Bridge the route makes its way along Dubbing Garth Lane passing a profusion of springtime wild flowers including campion, bugles, speedwell, forget-me-nots, buttercups and wild garlic. Crossing back over the older Isles Bridge the route heads back along the opposite bank to pass through the patchwork of meadows and field barns of Gunnerside Bottoms.

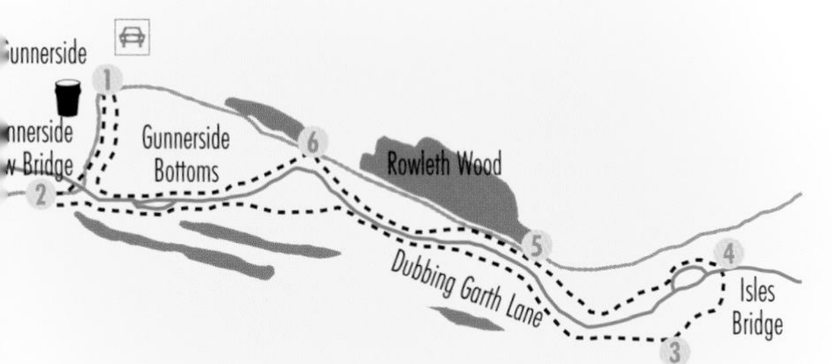

Level:

Length Miles and km: 4 ½ miles (7.4km)

Ascent feet and m: Negligible

Terrain: Clear paths and lanes throughout

Park and Start: Limited parking adjacent to Gunnerside Literary Institute GR950 982

Info: Refreshments from The Kings Head pub and Ghyll Tea Room in Gunnerside

1 Park next to the beck in the centre of the village and walk along the main road heading to the Gunnerside New Bridge over the Swale. Cross the Swale over the rising New Bridge and continue up the road as it swings around to the right and gently rises to give a fine view up the valley with Gunnerside Lodge prominent in the centre ground.

2 As the road levels out and turns to the right again take the lane to the left signed to Crackpot over the cattle grid. The lane immediately forks; take the left track along Dubbing Garth Lane through a gate down the bridleway with a fingerpost signed "BP Grinton 5 ½". The unsurfaced lane follows the line of the Swale downstream. The lane drops down to the valley bottom and proceeds with the Swale just over the bank on the left. Simply follow the lane through the hay meadows as it cuts off a bend in the Swale and then follows the riverbanks all the way to Haverdale House.

Gunnerside

Cow Parsley along Dubbing Garth Lane

3 Passing Haverdale House the lane regains a surface; continue straight on to join the road ahead. Turn left to walk down the quiet road towards Isles Bridge. A small bridge crosses over Haverdale Beck as Isles Bridge over the Swale comes into view. The road swings around to the left to go over the bridge.

4 Immediately over Isles Bridge take the fingerpost "Footpath" sign to the left through a narrow wall stile to pick up the path to return upstream. Initially keep to the path just next to the fence in front of Isles. The muddy path rises above the Swale, passes through some trees and then the way opens out along the meadows following the banks of the Swale. The path fords a stream before continuing though the meadows following a row of waymarkers. Respect this unique landscape by walking in single file through the hay meadows. The path crosses a footbridge over a stream and a stile into the next field as it passes a collection of buildings. Follow the footpath sign through a gated wall stile into the next meadow which heads towards the road beneath Rowleth Wood.

Dubbing Garth Lane

5 The path emerges to join the main valley road which can be busy at times. Keep your wits about you as you walk along the verge along the road. After a couple of hundred yards follow the "Public Footpath" fingerpost pointing to the path away from the road. The path now follows the river upstream through the woodland filled with the white blooms of wild garlic in the late spring. The path hugs the wooded banks of the Swale and proceeds over a series of stiles. Over one last stile and the route steeply rises on a

River Swale near Isles Bridge

stepped path away from the river back up to the road.

6 As soon as the road is reached go through the gate on the left to continue down a farm track back to the riverbank. Follow the path along the riverbank back to Gunnerside. As the river approaches the New Bridge keep strictly to the path following the riverbank – don't be tempted to stray into the adjacent fields. Just before the bridge and at a small stone building go through the metal gate and follow the path through the meadow to a narrow wall stile in the far corner. Cross the next pasture and follow the path back to the village.

Gunnerside Bottoms

At Gunnerside Bottoms, the intricate patchwork of vibrant green fields with dry stone wall boundaries and many field barns, create the classic image of the defining characteristic of Swaledale. Many species of wildflowers flourish in these ancient fields next to the Swale.

7 Banks of the Swale

A easy stroll along the Swale between Scabba Wath and Reeth Suspension bridges

This is the second of the pair of easy low-level riverbank strolls. This time starting just before the elegant Scabba Wath Bridge over the Swale. After a gentle rise on a narrow back lane, which gives a great view across the valley to the village of Healaugh on the lower slopes of the heather-topped Calver Hill, the route drops down to hug the riverbank all the way to the re-constructed Suspension Bridge on the fringes of Reeth. The return keeps to the riverbank all the way to Barney Beck, another of the Swale's tributaries, which has to forded on foot before a final short section along the busy B6270 main valley road.

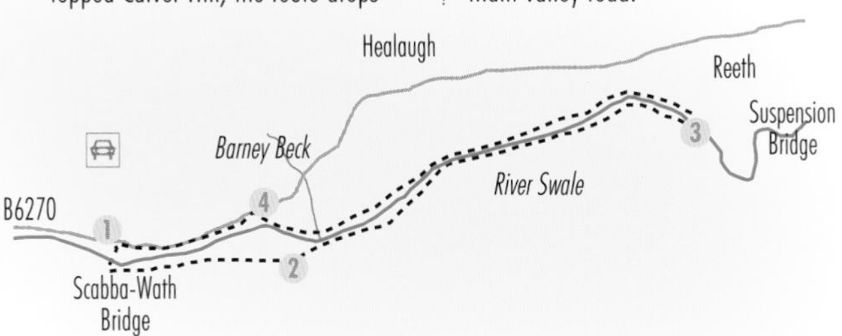

Level:

Length Miles and km: 3 ½ miles (5.8km)

Ascent feet and m: Negligible

Terrain: Riverside paths

Park and Start: Large layby at Parkhouse Farm on B6270 GR 006 984

Info: No facilities on route

Suspension bridge over the Swale near Reeth

1 Start from the large layby at Parkhouse Farm just to the west of Scabba Wath Bridge. Walk the 50 yards along the road heading towards Reeth and then turn right down the minor road signed to Askrigg to walk cross the Swale over Scabba Wath Bridge. Immediately over the bridge turn left to walk along the single track road signposted to Grinton. The road crosses a cattle grid to enter the Grinton Estate; continue walking along the road with bracken on either side. The road gently rises away from the river.

2 At a grit heap just before a telegraph pole a drystone wall veers away from the road to the left marked by a fingerpost

Scabba Wath Bridge over the Swale

The Swale is one of the fastest rising spate rivers in England – rising at a rate of 3 metres in 20 minutes. The current suspension bridge is almost identical to the original 'Swing Bridge', built in 1920 with community-raised funds, which was destroyed during flooding in 2000 when an uprooted tree smashed through.

"Footpath"; take the faint path beside the wall to continue walking downstream towards Reeth. Pass over a stile through the wall and the path continues on grass above the banks of

Calver Hill

the Swale. The green path proceeds along the level with the wall on the right with clear views across to Healaugh and Calver Hill on the opposite side of the valley. The path drops down the bank and goes through a gate beside the riverbank before proceeding to follow the riverbank. The wide and slow Swale now lazily makes its way along the dale. It's delightful easy walking along the tree lined riverside path. Whilst the OS maps show the right of way veering away from the riverbank the path on the ground continues to hug the riverbank all the way to the bridge. The suspension bridge across the Swale soon comes into view.

3 A finger post points the way over the bridge "Reeth ½ mile". Cross the bridge and immediately over the bridge turn left to follow the riverbank path on the opposite side of the Swale upstream heading back to the start. The path makes its way through the meadows bordering the river over a variety of stiles along the way and passes by the village of Healaugh on the right. Pass by a set of stepping stones over the Swale and continue on the riverbank path. The path reaches Barney Beck a tributary flowing into the Swale. Barney Beck has to be forded which can be challenging after periods of heavy rain when the beck is in spate.

4 The path follows the Swale through one large last field after crossing the beck to emerge onto

the B6270 main Swaledale road and all that is now required is to carefully walk back along the edge of the road back to the start some ½ mile distant. Keep a tight hold of young children and dogs whilst walking along this stretch of occasionally busy road.

Slopes of Calver Hill

Banks of the Swale

Stepping stones across the Swale

8 Old Gang and Surrender

An exploration of lead mining heritage with great views

Another chance to explore some more of Swaledale's lead mining heritage. This time to visit the spectacular remains of the Old Gang Smelt Mill deep in the heart of the mining fields north of the Swale. Four arched flues leave the back of the mill which combine into a single flue that goes up the slopes of Healaugh Side for nearly half a mile. The walk goes along Old Gang Beck whose waters were used to power both Old Gang and the nearby Surrender Mills before turning to head up Forefield Rake to pass by the summit of Great Pinseat, at just short of 2000 feet, the highest point reached in this collection of walks.

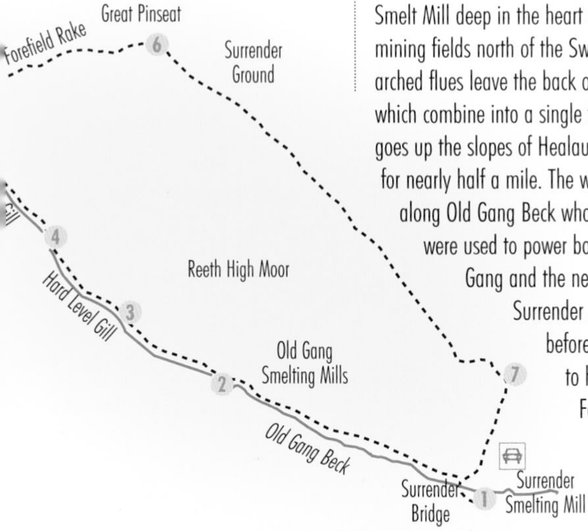

Great Pinseat
Forefield Rake
6
Surrender Ground
Gill
4
Reeth High Moor
Hard Level Gill
3
Old Gang Smelting Mills
2
7
Old Gang Beck
Surrender Bridge
1
Surrender Smelting Mill

Level:
Length Miles and km: 5 ¾ miles (9km)
Ascent feet and m: 1000 feet (300m)
Terrain: Miners roads and tracks
Park and Start: Off road at Surrender Bridge GR 989 998
Info: No facilities on route

Mine entrance - DO NOT ENTER

1 Start from Surrender Bridge where there is plenty of off road parking. Cross to the northern side of Surrender Bridge over Old Gang Beck and after 50 yards turn left onto the unsurfaced miners' track signed "BW Only No vehicles" onto the track which leads up to Old Gang Smelt Mill. The line of shelters on the opposite bank of the beck which appear shortly are a line of modern shooting butts for the grouse shooting season which starts on August 12th each year. The track drops down to the level of the beck as the remains of Old Gang Smelt Mill come into sight with the evidence of lead mining all around.

Surrender Bridge

2 The impressive remains of Old Gang Smelt Mill are soon reached with the restored chimney and the main flue heading up the hillside behind. Having taken a good look at the ruins of the smelt mill, pass the bridge on the left and continue on the track straight on up the valley which now starts to gently rise.

3 The track forks at the bridge just past Hard Level Force; take the right hand fork to continue heading up the valley alongside Hard Level Gill up to Level House Bridge.

Old Gang Smelt Mill

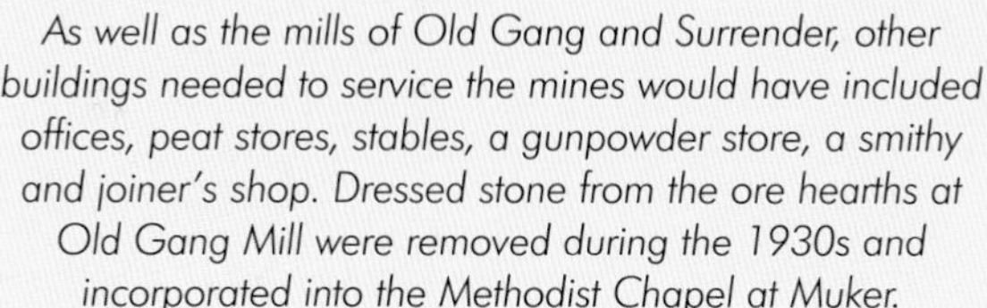

As well as the mills of Old Gang and Surrender, other buildings needed to service the mines would have included offices, peat stores, stables, a gunpowder store, a smithy and joiner's shop. Dressed stone from the ore hearths at Old Gang Mill were removed during the 1930s and incorporated into the Methodist Chapel at Muker.

Mine level entrance

The mine track gently rises uphill amidst desolate moorland with heather-covered slopes which are a riot of purple colour in late summer.

4 The impressive Level House Bridge is soon reached where the track forks again, and again take the right hand track which now heads up besides Flincher Gill. The track passes the ruins of Level House. As Flincher Gill peters out the evidence of lead mining is all around passing the scar that is North Rake Hush across the moorland on the left. Long abandoned spoil heaps and tips abound amongst the heather. The track crosses over the gill and passes a pair of restored mine entrances – do not go in! The track crosses back over the gill just before reaching a gate.

Summit marker

5 Go through the gate where the track swings around to the right to go up Forefield Rake on the way towards the top of Great Pinseat. The track up Forefield Rake is a scene of desolation, mining waste land and wilderness. As you walk up Forefield Rake take a look back to also see Friarfold Rake across the valley and again North Rake Hush. At the top of the route a summit marker has been erected and the path continues now heading south east with extensive views to the Vale of York. The top of Great Pinseat is just over the wall on the left if you want to take in the true summit.

6 Passing a spoil heap the track the track starts to very gradually lose height as it starts to head back to the start; Fremington Edge and Arkengarthdale are in view to the front left with the triangular-shaped Calver Hill in the foreground. The track passes a large sheepfold on

Shooting butt

Left: Heather-covered Calver Hill

the left and the rusted remains of a long abandoned van on the right. It's a long gentle descent now down the slopes of Great Pinseat heading back towards the road with Calver Hill dominating the view to the front. A line of traditional stone-built shooting butts are passed on the right as the track approaches the road.

With the road just in sight the track swings sharply to the left to descend to meet the road with lower Swaledale in view.

7 The surfaced road across the moor is reached and all that's required is to turn right to walk back along the road to Surrender Bridge and the start. There are outstanding views of the purple moorland in late summer. The road crosses the flue from Surrender Mill and the road drops steeply down to Surrender Bridge. Finally take the opportunity to explore the remains of Surrender Bridge Smelt Mill before making your way back to the car.

Surrender Smelt Mill

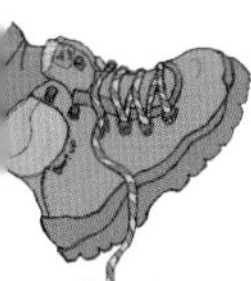

9 Arkle Beck

A trip up the lower stretches of Arkle Beck above Reeth

Arkengarthdale is the principle subsidiary valley of Swaledale, joining the Swale at Reeth, the dales' largest centre of population.

Reeth was already established well enough to be mentioned in the *Domesday Book* and today the triangular village green is surrounded by a number of hostelries which are still busy on market day. The route follows the course of Arkle Beck upstream on the eastern valley side almost as far as Langthwaite returning through the fields along the slopes of Calver Hill. A number of short sections on the walk can become wet underfoot after heavy rain.

Langthwaite
Hoggs House
Fremington Edge
Arkle Town
West Raw Croft Farm
Castle Farm
Calver Hill
Cuckoo Hill
Arkle Beck
Reeth
1 2 3 4 5 6 7

Level: 🥾🥾
Length Miles and km: 6 miles (10km)
Ascent feet and m: 750 feet (225m)
Terrain: Undulating route on green paths
Park and Start: Reeth Village Green
Info: Various pubs, cafés, hotels and tea shops in Reeth

Arkle Beck from the footbridge

1 Park next to the village green in the middle of Reeth. Head down to the bottom of the village along the road towards the bridge over Arkle Beck. Pass the village store at the bottom of the hill and continue walking along the roadside towards the bridge. Cross the bridge over the Arkle and then on the left hand side of the road go through the gated wall stile following the sign "Footpath" to join an unsurfaced track which starts to head up Arkengarthdale. Approaching the first field barn on the right go straight on through the field keeping the drystone wall on your left hand side. At a stand of trees the way is pointed away from the beck heading up the hillside, through two pastures and passing a field barn heading up towards Cuckoo Hill.

2 Go through the wall at the top of the second meadow to arrive at a clear track. Turn left following the "Public Footpath" sign to continue up the valley, but first turn back to take a look down onto the village of Reeth before continuing up the valley. Given the number of rabbits hereabout "The Warren" would be a more appropriate name

Looking back towards Reeth

Looking down onto Arkle Beck

than Cuckoo Hill. It's easy walking along the track up the valley with great views across to Calver Hill on the opposite side of the valley. With occasional glimpses of the beck down on the left the track passes through the hawthorn scrub and trees of the woodland on the way to Castle Farm.

3 At a disused pair of gateposts the route forks; take the "Public Bridleway" veering off to the right up the hillside for the higher level route along the valley. The green path gently rises up the hillside through the upper edge of the wood. Continuing to rise the path skirts around the upper edge of the wood before levelling off just above Castle Farm where the view up the valley opens out and the way proceeds up the valley keeping in line with the drystone wall up to Hoggs House. With the river meandering in the valley bottom the path undulates along the valley with occasional reassurance from yellow waymarker posts.

4 Upon reaching Hoggs House, go through the yellow waymarked gate through the fence just before the cottage. The path drops down around the back of the house and then continues up the

Arkle Beck

valley on a clear track to meet the river at the first of a number of bridges over Arkle Beck. This could be a short cut back to the return route, over the beck and the farm track up to West Raw Croft Farm and then pick up the return route at Point 6. Otherwise continue on the green path beside the river upstream through the riverside pastures. Keep to the path which hugs the riverside ignoring a path up to the right to Storthwaite Hall. The path crosses an iron footbridge over Slei Gill just before entering Arkle Beck. Continue upstream on the riverside path, passing the remains of lead mining activity. The path enters a tunnel in the lead mining remains before passing into woodland where a sign marks the way "FP Langthwaite". The path along the edge of the woods steers away from the Beck and becomes a track. This unsurfaced track drops down to emerge at a stone building just before the second wooden footbridge over the beck; cross over here.

Arkengarthdale from Castle Farm

5 Immediately over the bridge; turn left and over a stile to pick up the beck side path for the return along the opposite bank. Follow the clear path beside the beck

downstream towards Reeth. The clear path gradually veers away from the river rising slightly up the hillside to proceed through the fields through a series of stiles with Fremington Edge on the opposite side of the valley in view. As the way becomes unclear on the ground a fingerpost helpfully points the way forward to Reeth. After dropping down a field and through a gate the way proceeds besides a wall on the left.

6 The path arrives at West Rawcroft Farm, go straight on in front of the farm buildings and through a gate to continue through the meadows. The path rises above East Rawcroft Farm, crosses a stream

Though the tunnel!

and continues through the rough pasture.

7 As the path approaches Arkle Beck again at a junction of paths a signpost shows the way up a farm track "FP Reeth". Go through a gate next to a barn and take the green path straight on through the meadows away from the farm track. The path goes through a number of small meadows through a variety of stiles and gaps in the enclosing walls. Castle Farm can be seen again on the opposite side of the valley. Approaching the outskirts of Reeth the waymarked path veers to the right to join the road where all that remains is the unavoidable stretch along the road down through Reeth back to the start.

Arkengarthdale, better known for its lead mining heritage was originally mined for coal as early as 1285, when the mine which was owned by the Earl of Richmond turned a profit of £4. By 1485 a coal mine "not occupied" was still parcel of the manor.

Arkle Beck from the footbridge

10 Grinton Smelt Mill

A last chance to visit Swaledale's mining heritage

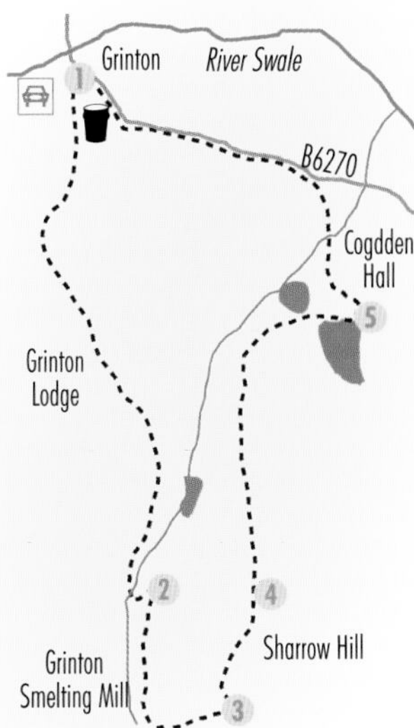

This short walk leads to the best preserved lead smelt mill in the Yorkshire Dales National Park. The buildings date from around 1820, although lead had been mined and processed on the site for at least the previous six centuries. The mill was last used for smelting lead in 1886. The high level of preservation is partly due to its subsequent agricultural use including the installation of a sheep dip by local farmers. The two furnaces were originally water powered by a 7m diameter waterwheel in the diverted water-course. The flue from the mill goes straight up Sharrow Hill where a triple-arched lime kiln is to be found.

Level:
Length Miles and km: 3 ½ miles (5.6km)
Ascent feet and m: 650 feet (200m)
Terrain: Steady climb up to Sharrow Hill
Park and Start: Roadside St Andrew's church, Grinton GR 046 984
Info: Refreshments from The Bridge Inn, Grinton

Lime kiln on Sharrow Hill

St Andrew's church, Grinton

1 Park in the village of Grinton, where there is limited roadside parking outside St Andrew's church opposite The Bridge Inn. Start by walking up the Redmire and Leyburn Road. There is close to a mile of uphill walking up this quiet road taking the usual care whilst road walking. After a stiff climb out of the back of Grinton the road crosses a cattle grid onto the moors and the road continues to steadily rise. The road passes the rather austere looking Grinton Lodge which now serves as of the few remaining YHA hostels in the dale. The road continues to gently rise now with open moorland on either side. As the road levels off the limestone scar edging the top of Sharrow Hill is seen to the front left. Cogden Gill flows along to the left of the road. Cross the bridge over Cogden Gill and the road turns sharply round to the left.

2 Almost immediately the wide unsurfaced track to take you up beside Cogden Gill to the smelt mill appears on the right signed; "Bridleway No Vehicles". This old miners' track continues up the gill with the stream now on the right across the heather-covered moorland. Shortly the restored buildings of Grinton Lead Smelt Mill come into

Grinton Lodge

view. There is a series of interpretation panels inside the main building. Having taken a good look around the disused smelt mill, continue by following the path beside the smelt flue straight up the hillside up to the top of Sharrow Hill. An alternative is to continue following the miners' track which eventually arrives at the mine head on the top of the moor and then walk along the ridge of Sharrow Hill back to the top of the flue – however paths are very clear underfoot along the top of the ridge. There are indications of the lead mining heritage all around.

3 Reaching the top of the flue continue upwards for a few more yards and then bear left to visit the true top of Sharrow Hill. The view opens out down to Reeth and along Arkengarthdale and the return path across the moor can also be clearly seen below. To avoid a scramble down the front of Sharrow Hill head back to the top of the flue, follow it back down for 30 yards to pick up a clear green path to the right which heads around the front of the hill passing the limestone quarry on the hill and an impressive triple-arched lime kiln. The wide green path goes around the upper slopes of Sharrow Hill heading

Cogden Gill

for the road below. The path drops down to the road.

4 Cross straight over the road and take the green track "Bridleway" through the gate straight on. This is easy walking gently descending across the heather covered grouse moors with extensive views along Swaledale and Arkengarthdale. The path passes through a gate through a drystone wall and then forks, take the left hand fork which continues downhill looking down onto the village of Grinton with Reeth in the distance. The path meets up with a wall which swings around to the right continuing to lose height heading towards Cogden Hall. The path passes above Cogden Hall with a plantation of fir trees on the right.

The castle-like Grinton Lodge is a former shooting lodge high on the side of Swaledale, built in the early 19th century by James Fenton of Doncaster, owner of the Grinton Manor Estate. It was sold to the Youth Hostels Association in 1948 for £5,500.

5 Approaching the end of the plantation the track forks; take the left hand fork which swings back round to descend to Cogden Hall. The track goes past the farm buildings at Cogden Hall and emerges onto a walled lane. Turn left along the lane which emerges onto the busy B6270 main valley road. Simply turn left and walk beside the road on the wide verges back to Grinton and the start.

Miners' track up to the mill

Grinton Smelt MIll

Smelt mill flue

Reeth